Yes! You can create...
A Memory Bear!

by Deborah Rawles

With easy step by step instructions for beginners.

Thanks to:

God

Mum

Isabella

Yes you can create a memory bear.

A lot of people who can sew and craft have family members who do the same. They grow up seeing their elders work and take it in. But, what if you don't have that? What if you have never sewn a stitch in your life and would not know where to start? It can seem impossible when you have never been shown. In this book you will be guided through each step, so you will be able to create a whole bear. It may seem like a huge challenge but, when it is broken down into the smallest of steps, it becomes so much easier to do. You will be amazed when you have steadily gone through the easy steps and have created a bear by yourself.

We had several school jumpers that were too small and wondered what we could do with them. They held so many memories. I decided to make a teddy bear from one and it was so loved, that at Christmas the teachers each received one. It felt a little nerve wracking giving something handmade as a thank you gift but the reactions were wonderful. One teacher said it was the best gift she had ever been given! So, whether the teddy bear is a keepsake for yourself or a gift for someone, you will be proud of what you have achieved. There is something extra special about someone saying they love it and asking where you got it and you being able to reply "I made it myself".

At the back of the book you will find the pattern pages. They may look complicated, if you have never used a pattern before, but I can assure you each step will be simple and easy to understand. The pattern has been designed to be the easiest to put together. I would recommend not setting yourself a deadline for when you need to have completed your teddy bear. Just enjoy the simple steps and don't rush it.

We will start with one of the most important steps when sewing and that is choosing the right fabric. If you have a beautiful memory silk shirt, pop it back in the drawer. If you have some thick denim memory jeans, pop them in the drawer next to the silk shirt. The bear in the picture is made from a sweatshirt fabric that does not fray. Fraying is when you cut the fabric and all the threads start hanging out. Sweater fabric is good to sew, as is cotton T-shirting (that your T-shirt is made out of). Do not use anything knitted because when it is cut, the wool will fall apart. Your fabric will not be see-through, not slippery (like a satin nightdress) and not really thick because they are tricky to sew. It can be done but it is hard and we are taking the simplest and easier route in this book, so you can succeed. If you are not sure if your memory fabric is going to work, take it to a shop that sells fabric and tell them what your plan is. You will need to go there anyway to buy some supplies.

The pattern.

At the back of the book, there are the pattern pages. You will need to cut out each piece. Take your time. It is not a race. There is no prize for being the fastest. Carefully cut along each outline, as accurately as you can.

When you have finished, lay all the pieces on to your memory fabric to check you have enough to work with.

Keep all of the arrows running the same way. On the front and backs of garments the arrows will point down, from the neck down to the bottom. On sleeves, the arrows will point from the shoulder down to the cuff. If you are working with fur, the arrows point the way your hand moves as you stroke it flat.

If you are hoping to include a logo from a jumper or cardigan, make sure it fits in one of the Front Body pieces with a gap around it for sewing the pieces together.

Are you happy with your choice of fabric?

Do you have enough of it to cut out every piece?

If you can answer yes to each of these questions then you are ready to start.

You will need:

- Your choice of memory fabric.
- Thread to match your fabric colour.
- Sewing needle.
- Sharp fabric scissors.
- Stuffing.
- Black cross stitch floss that you use for the nose and mouth.
- Large eye needle.
- 2 teddy bear safety eyes 10mm, whichever colour you like and backs.
- 2cm by 60cm Ribbon for the teddy bears bow, your choice of colour.
- A black ballpoint pen, fabric pattern pen or tailors chalk. Not Felt tip pens or permanent marker pens as the ink spreads out on most fabrics.
- A ruler or tape measure.
- A pencil.
- Possibly a needle threader.
- Pins.

Creating the pattern pieces.

If you are using an old garment to make your bear, you will need to cut off the extra pieces. You may wish to use a less sentimental item for your first bear.

Cut off the sleeves and cut the fabric as close to the stitching joining it together as you can, to save fabric.

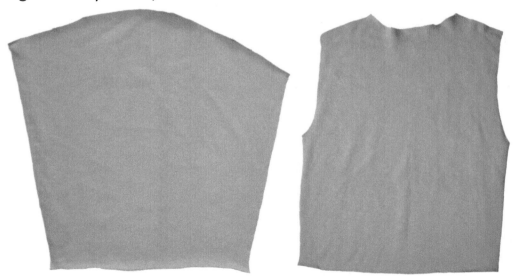

This is a sleeve and the back of a jumper, after the extras have been cut off. Lay your fabric out on a hard surface.
Next, lay all of your cut out pattern pieces on to the fabric. You may need to move them around to fit them all in, just make sure all of the arrows point in

the correct direction for your fabric and that no pieces overlap. You can choose to include any special details on the fabric and avoid any snags, marks or fades. If you have a school logo, make sure you place the front body piece up the correct way, so it will be on the front of the finished bear.

Try to use as little of the fabric as you can. Place the pieces close together just in case you need to cut any extra pieces out again and you will have some left over fabric to use.

Using a black ballpoint pen, fabric pattern pen or tailors chalk, carefully draw around each piece. You will need to hold each piece firmly down so it cannot move and use little strokes of the pen, otherwise it will drag the fabric along. Take your time to get it just right. Slow and steady.

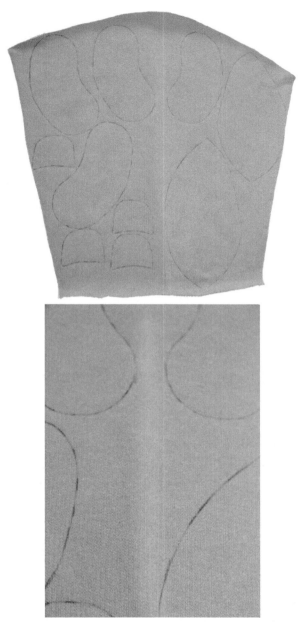

This picture shows how easy it is to work around faded patches.

Very carefully cut along the lines. Allow yourself plenty of time and even come back to it later instead of rushing it and getting it wrong. Mind your fingers. If you have the fabric resting on your lap, be careful that your clothes do not get envolved in the cutting. It's easily done. This can take a couple of days to complete.

When you have finished, you will have 25 pieces.

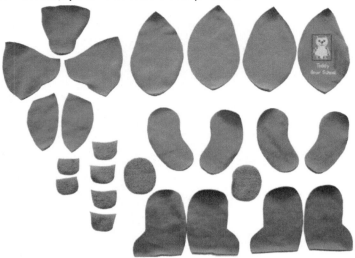

If you are using sweater fabric, you can turn over the ear, tail and foot pieces to their bobbly side.

Layout the paper pattern pieces in their original groups:

- Arms (4)
- Back of body and tail (4)
- Front of body (2)
- Head and ears (9)
- First leg and foot pad (3)
- Second leg and foot pad (3)

Then lay the cut fabric pieces on to them, to check you have every piece and so you can see which piece is which. It may help to pin them together.

Congratulations! You have completed your teddy bear pattern pieces.

Constructing your bear.

Let's start with an arm.

You will need:

- Two pattern pieces Arm 1 and Arm 2
- Matching sewing thread
- A small eye needle
- Scissors

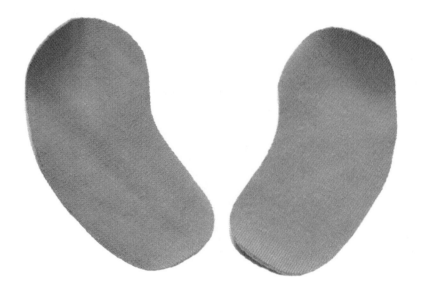

Take your two pattern pieces and place them so that the correct side of the fabric is facing up and the inside of the fabric is facing down. This is called the "right side up". The inside of the fabric is known as the "wrong" side.

Turn over the one on the left.

And place it on top of the other one.
You are now ready to begin the first stitching of your teddy bear.

Pull a 50cm (20 inch) length of thread, that matches the colour of your fabric, from the reel and cut it off. Pick up the thread close to the end in your best hand. Take your smaller eyed needle, in the hand you are not so good with, and push the end of thread through it. The end of the thread will need to be cut well and not fluffy or it will be really hard to thread the needle. Also you may need glasses and definitely good lighting. When you have successfully threaded the needle, pull it to about halfway along the thread.

Next you are going to tie the thread together. Put the two ends together and make a loop.

Put the two ends through the loop and pull tight.

Cut off the extra, close to the knot.

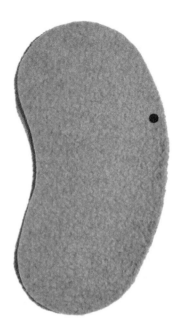

Minding your fingers, push the needle down through the two layers of fabric, (roughly in the position of the dot shown) all the way through.

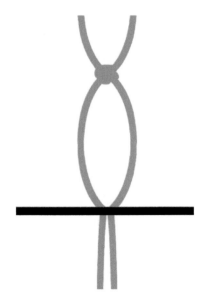

Pull the thread through most of the way but not all.

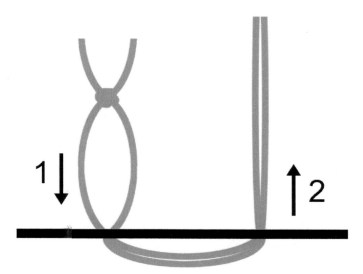

Move the needle along just a bit, to create your first stitch, and push it back up through the fabric. Don't pull it tight just yet.

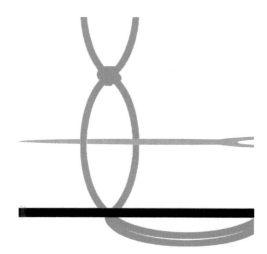

Push the needle through the thread that you left sticking up, just under the knot, making sure not to catch the point of the needle through the thread. It needs to go only through the gap.

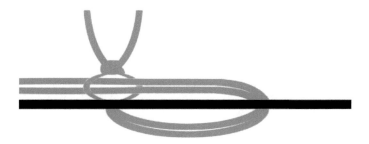

When you pull it tight, it creates the perfect anchor for the thread, so it cannot come undone. You will use this technique every time you start a new line of stitching.

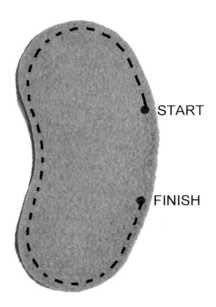

START

FINISH

Continue going in (down through the two layers of fabric) and out (up) in small stitches about ½ cm away from the edges. This is called a running stitch and is the most used stitch in sewing. You will need to stop 4cm (1 ¾ inches) from where you started. Each stitch does not have to be exactly the same length as the others, just as long as they are quite small it is fine. If at any time you get the thread in a tangle or something does not go to plan, just carefully cut the stitching only, remove the thread and begin again. Next, tie off your line of stitching and cut the thread. Finish your first running stitch with an up stitch, so the thread and needle are not underneath.

The next pictures show the thread as one line to make it clearer but yours will be two.

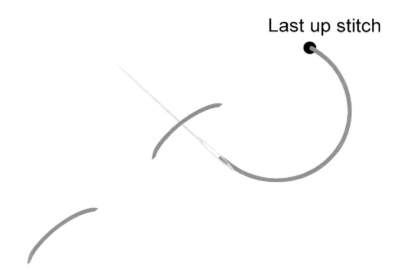

Last up stitch

Tuck the needle under the last full stitch you made on the top and loop the length of thread around.

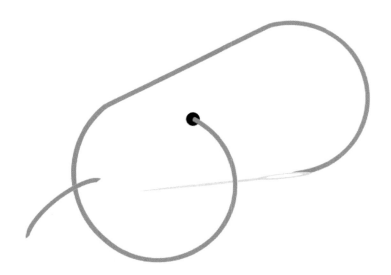

Run the needle under and through the loop you have just created two times and pull it tight to create a knot. Repeat the process by catching the needle under your last full stitch, looping the thread around, tucking the needle through the loop and pulling tight. Not too tight or you could snap the thread. Cut off the extra thread near to the knot. Congratulations! You have just completed your first line of stitching. This running stitch can be used to make endless items and make repairs on clothes whose seems have come apart.

Turn your bear's arm in the right way, by pushing it through the gap you left in the stitching.

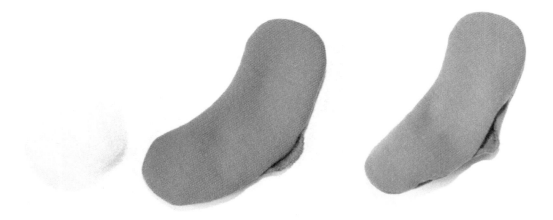

Tear off some stuffing and roll it between the palms of your hands to create a ball. Push it in through the hole and all the way to one end.

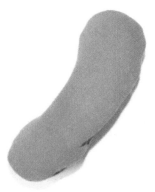

Do the same but push it to the opposite end. Repeat this until the bears arm is full. You want it to be full but not really hard. Your teddy bear needs to be cuddly.

Now it is time to sew up the gap. Once you have successfully completed these steps, you will have all the skills you need to complete the whole bear. Let's just remind ourselves what you will be able to create.

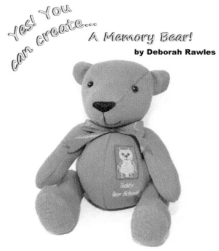

Yes! You can create...
A Memory Bear!
by Deborah Rawles

With easy step by step instructions for beginners.

We need to learn a slightly different stitch called a Slip Stitch. It's an invisible stitch that cannot be seen when completed. Some of the pictures show a white thread, so it can be seen more easily, but you will be using your thread that matches your fabric. Firstly, create your anchor stitch as shown.

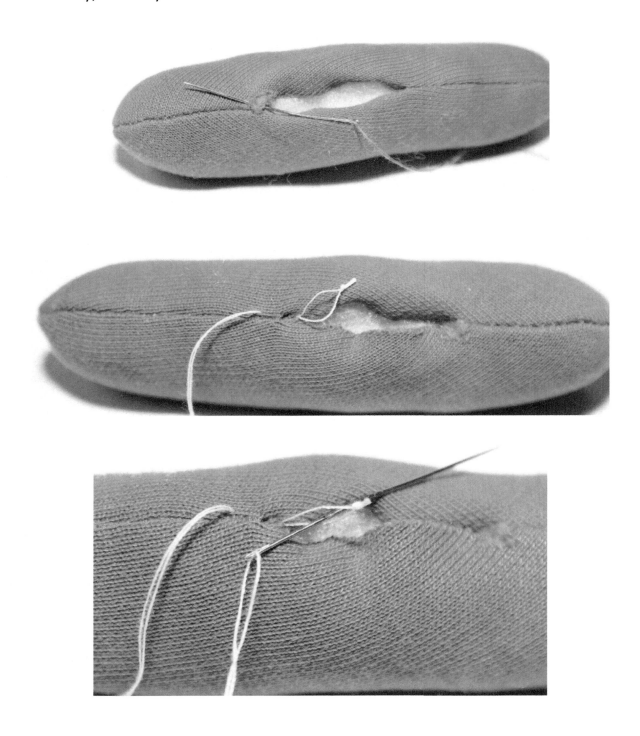

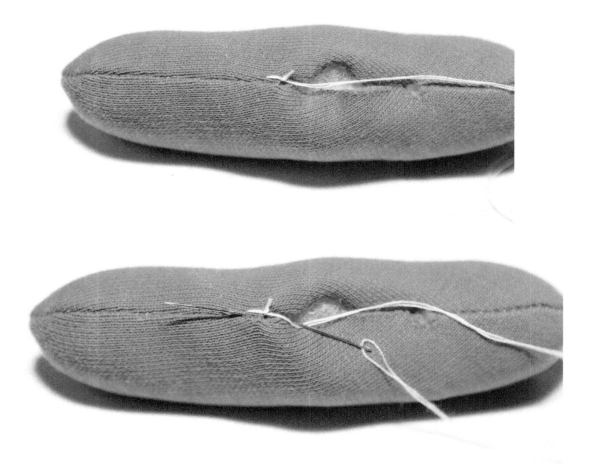

And then come up back through from inside the arm to the start of your stitch line. This way you can hide the Anchor Stitch with the Slip Stitch you are about to learn.

Slip Stitch is the same as running stitch, except instead of the stitches being in a straight line, the two pieces of fabric each get one stitch. It alternates one stitch for one side and one for the other. It goes like this.

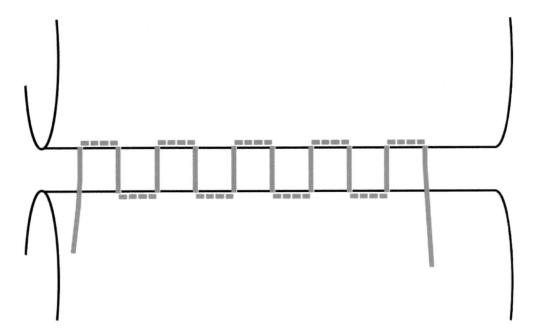

The dotted lines are the underside of the fabric. As you can see, it is one stitch one side then one stitch the other side. When it is pulled tight, the two pieces of fabric are pulled together and the stitch disappears.

Here is the first stitch after your Anchor Stitch.

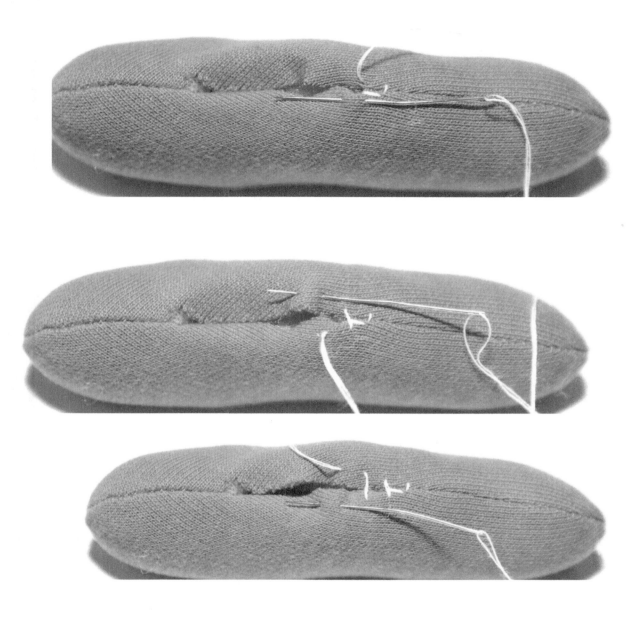

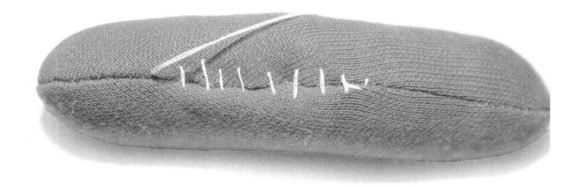

Here is what it will look like after you have worked your way along the length of the opening.

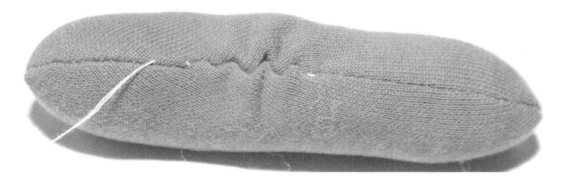

Pull the thread, to gather the seam, but not too much or it will pucker up. This is easily fixed by gently pulling each end of the opening. Finish off the line of stitching with the tying off technique you used earlier.

You have completed your bears arm. Repeat the steps above to make the second arm.

Now, take a look at what you have created. Just by changing the shape of the two pattern pieces and with different fabrics, you can make all sorts of things. This arm you have just made, in green material is a Pickle decoration they use at Christmas in Germany. If you were to cut two heart shaped pieces and add a ribbon loop, you have a lovely decoration for all year.

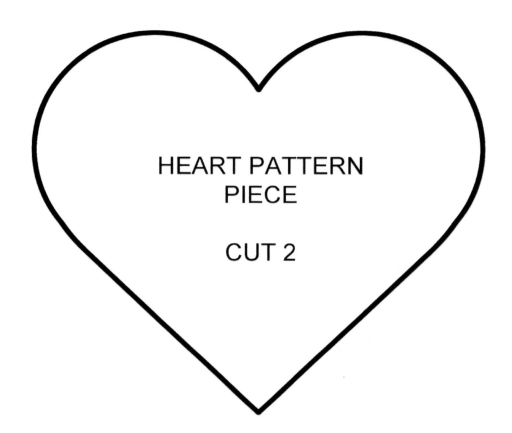

HEART PATTERN
PIECE

CUT 2

You could cut 2 heart shapes from some other fabric. This pattern is at the back of the book.

Fold a length of ribbon and place it on top of one of the heart shapes.

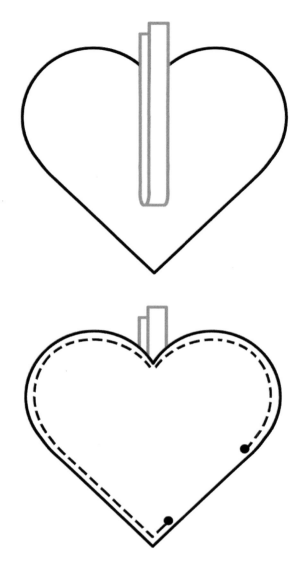

Place the other piece on top, wrong side up, and stitch around it. Exactly like you did with the bear's arm. When you turn it in the right way, stuff it and stitch up the opening, you have a lovely decoration. Before stitching it up, you could add some dry Lavender to make a closet pomander. Now you can create a pattern and sew it, you can make whatever you like.

Making the legs.

Each one of your bears legs are made from 3 pieces.

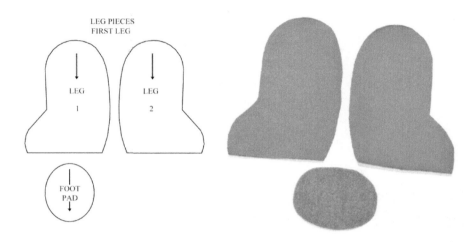

Take the Leg 1 and Leg 2 pieces and lay one right side up and the other on top of it, wrong side up.

You will need to complete two lines of stitching. The first line starts at the 1 with the arrow and ends at the second 1. Tie off your thread. Leave a gap big enough for stuffing. Start the second line at the 2 with the arrow and end it at the second 2. Tie it off. It is very easy to just keep sewing with the first thread and forget to leave the gap. You will need to stop and start at the place shown, or your bear will have flat legs. Remember not to worry if anything doesn't go just right first time. Just carefully cut the thread and start again.

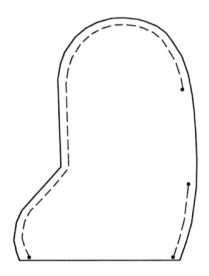

It should look like this when you have finished.

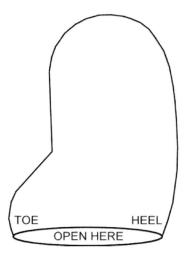

TOE   HEEL

OPEN HERE

Open the bottom of the two pieces.

Place the Foot Pad on to the gap with the oval shape, running from toe to heel. The sweater fabric has a bobbly side the wrong way up. It has been placed upside down so that the finished bear's foot pad will have a different look to the rest of the fabric. If you decide to do this, make sure you do the same with both foot pads so they match.

The foot pad can move around a bit while you are stitching it in position, so it may help you to pin it in place or to just stitch these points before starting to stitch the whole foot pad.

This time you sew a complete line of stitching, starting and finishing at the same place. You do not need to leave a gap for stuffing. Make sure the edges of the bear's foot pad lines up with the leg, all the way round.

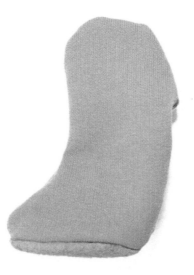

Turn it in the right way, through the gap you cleverly left earlier.

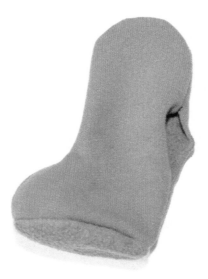

Make sure you push the stuffing right down to the bottom of the toes,

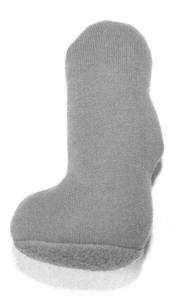

and fill out the foot shape, before filling up the rest of the leg. Sew up the gap and you have completed your first bear's leg! Repeat the steps above, to create the second leg.

The bear's body.

When you have completed this part, you will end up with something like a ball with a little tail. Let's start with the front of the bear.

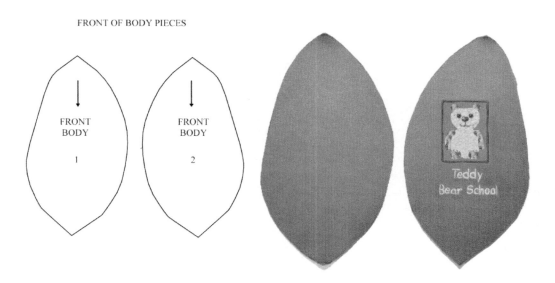

FRONT OF BODY PIECES

You will need the Front Body pieces 1 and 2. Place the pieces as shown, turn over piece 1.

Place piece 1 on top of piece 2, so the wrong side is facing up. You will notice that the left edge has a smoother curve than the right.

Stitch together the smooth left edge and put this to one side for now.

Take the two tail pieces and sandwich inside the fabric you want to be shown on your finished bear. In this case the wrong side has been used because it is bobbly and it will give a bit of interest to the finished bear.

Run a line of stitching as shown.

And turn the tail in the right way.

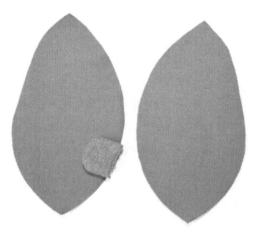

Place the Back Body pieces as shown and put the unstitched edge of the bears tail, you have just made, in the position shown in the picture.

The tail needs to stick out of the sandwich just a bit.

Again you are stitching along the smooth curved edge but, the same as with the back of the bear's legs, you are leaving a gap. You will be running two separate lines of stitching, starting from the bottom. Make sure to catch the tail in with the bottom line of stitching.

Turn it in the right way.

And slot it in to the Front Body pieces, you put to one side earlier, like a hand in a pocket. You will now have a 4 pieces of fabric sandwich.

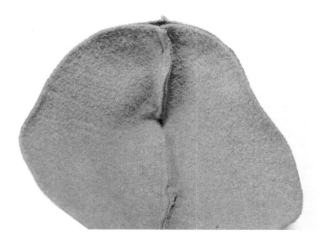

Put your hand in between the 4 layers, so you have 2 layers each side of your hand, and open it up. You will have 2 layered half a ball shape. Make sure the "right" sides of the fabric are inside these 2 layers before beginning the stitching.

Stitch all the way around the circle, remembering to keep the two edges in line as you go. It may help you to pin the top and the sides in place before you start.

Turn the body in the right way, through the gap you left yourself earlier, and stuff it. The body will need to be quite firm, as it holds up the head. Lastly, sew up the gap with Slip Stitch.

As you look at the bear's body you have just created, you can see how easy it is to make a 3 dimensional shape like a Rugby Ball or American Football. Again with different fabric and no tail you can make a ball. There is the pattern piece for a Rugby Ball or American Football at the back of the book.

The head.

At this point your teddy bear should have: two arms, two legs and a body. All stuffed, with the gaps sewn up and none of them attached to each other. Next, it is time to use all the remaining pattern pieces. 9 pieces do look like a lot but it will all make sense as you go through the steps.

Take two of the Bear Ears pieces and sew them together in exactly the same way you did with the Bear's tail pieces. The bobbly side has been used inside, again to match the tail and foot pads.

Sew them together and turn in the right way. They do not need padding unless you have very floppy fabric.

Repeat this with the other two ear pieces. You now only have 5 pattern pieces to go!

Take the two back of head pieces and place them next to each other, wrong sides down, so they match the picture.

Turn over the one on the left and lay it on top of the other one, so they line up.

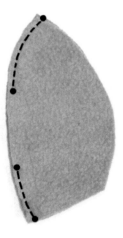

Run two separate lines of stitching along the curved edge. Again, this leaves a gap for you to stuff the bear's head when you have completed it. When you have done this, you have made the back of the bear's head. Put this to one side for later.

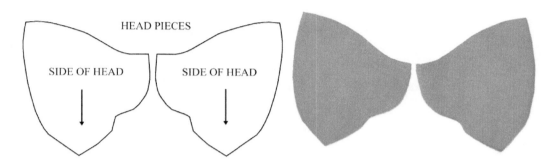

HEAD PIECES

SIDE OF HEAD

SIDE OF HEAD

Take the two Side of Head pieces and place them right side up.

This time, turn the right hand piece over and place it on top of the other so the edges line up.

Only stitch along the bottom right hand line as shown. The bear's nose is pointing to the right. Open out the joined pieces and lay them with the bear's nose pointing away from you and the "right" side of the fabric is facing up.

Take the Top of Head and Nose piece. Lay it on top of the others, wrong side up, so the point lines up with the bear's nose point.

Run a short line of stitching to secure the nose point. It is important to do this or your bear could end up with a wonky nose.

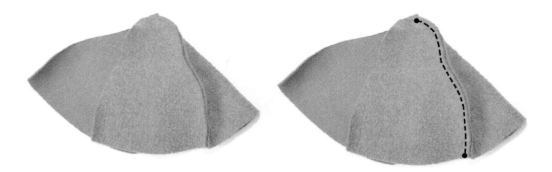

Sew the top right edge of the bear's face, to the right side of the bear's nose, as shown.

Do the same with the left side.

Open it up.

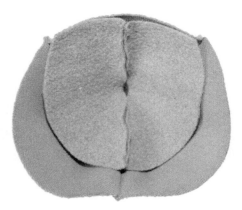

Take the back of the bear's head piece (that you stitched together earlier and put to one side). Lay it so the top edges line up and the wrong side of the fabric faces up.

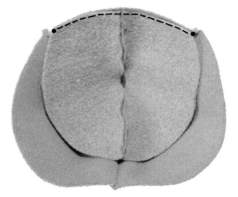

Sew along the top edge.

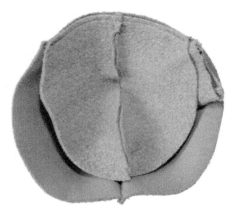

Take one of the bear's ears and slot it between the two layers of fabric, in the position shown.

Just like the tail you added to the bear's bottom earlier, you need the edges sticking out a little.

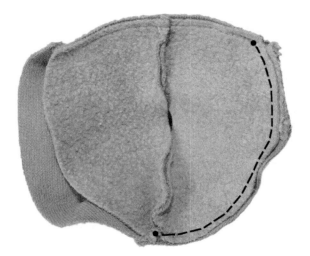

This next part may take slightly longer than a normal line of stitching because of the shapes that need to join up. Take your time. Pinning it before you start may help you. Start your line of stitching at the top and sew in the ear first, as it is easier. Make sure that the bottom points meet up.

Repeat with the other side, remembering to add the ear. Turn the bear's head in the right way, through the hole you left.

Adding the bear's face detail.

First you will place the eyes.

Measure down from the bear's ear, along the seam, 4cm or just over 1 ½ inches. Place a pin in this position. You can hold your bear's eye up to it and see if you like how it will look. You may need to move the pin further out from the seam. Whatever you decide to do, do exactly the same on the other side of the face.

Look at the positioning of the two pins to double check that they are symmetrical, like a mirror of each other.

When you are happy with the position, gently push a small hole exactly where the pin is using scissors. You do not want a large hole. It needs to be just big enough to push the shank of the eye through. Push the eye in and push the safety back on, inside the bear's head with your fingers through the gap at the back of the head.

Do the same with the other eye. Make sure the eyes are securely on and cannot be pulled off.

Stuff the bear's head, starting with the nose and then sew up the back of the head with your slip stitch.

Congratulations! Your bear should now have: 2 arms, 2 legs, a body and a head. All stuffed with the gaps stitched up. You can really see how cute your bear will look when it's finished.

A lot of crafters and painters struggle with finishing off a project. They do a lot of work on it and, then when the end is in sight, they stop and start a new project. They leave a string of unfinished projects behind them. Craft is like running a long race in a competition. When you get near the end, you have to give it some extra energy and sprint to the finish line. Think of the sense of achievement you will have when you finally hold the bear you made yourself!

Next you will join the legs to the body.

Attaching the legs, arms and head.

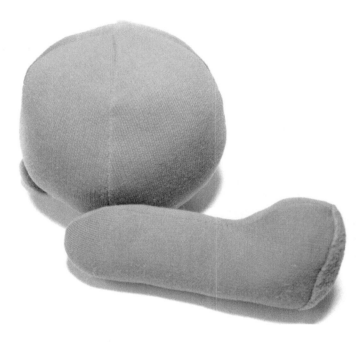

Place the body side on and rest one leg against it. Look to see where the leg touches the body. As you look, press the leg into the body a bit. Around the area that touches, you will run your slip stitch so it holds on the leg and cannot be seen when it is finished.

Begin with your anchor stitch in the middle of the area of leg that was touching the body.

The first stitch enters the fabric next to your anchor stitch and the needle comes out at the edge of the area that was touching the bear.

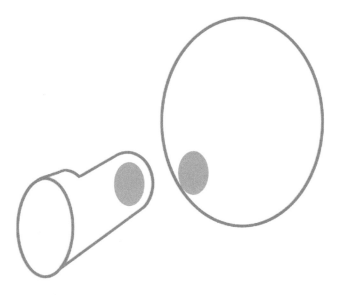

You are joining these two shaded areas together.

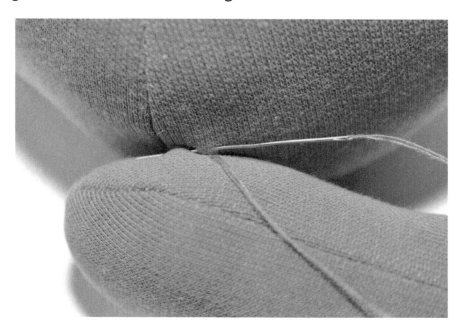

So, exactly as you did for sewing up the gaps with the slip stitch, you are joining the leg to the bear. Alternating, one stitch for the leg and one for the body. Make sure you keep the leg in the correct position as it will dangle around a bit as you make the first few stitches.

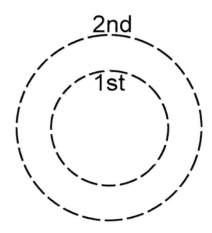

If, when you have sewn all the way around, you find the leg is too dangly, just run a second line of stitching in a wider circle so more of the leg is touching the bear and there is more to hold it on.

Repeat the process with the second leg. Make sure it is in the same mirror position as the first leg as you have sewn.

The tops of the arms are level with the top of the body. The bear's hands rest just outside each leg. Take your time and if you are not happy with the position, when you have sewn them on, carefully snip <u>just</u> the thread and start again. The finished bear is what matters, nobody knows if you make a mistake and do it again, to get it just right.

You should now have a headless bear. It might be worth keeping this sight away from children, until you have attached its head.

Next sew on the bear's head. You will need a wider circle of slip stitch and to make sure that the face points forward as you stitch round. Place the head on and decide how it looks best before starting to stitch.

Sewing the nose.

You will need:

- 3 pins
- A pencil
- Black cross stitch floss thread
- A large eyed needle
- Scissors

Take the 3 pins and place them at the 3 points of your bear's nose, making sure the top two are level and match each other.

You can wrap some of the black floss around the pins to get a clearer idea of how your bear will look when his nose is on before drawing the pencil line.

When you have drawn on the pencil triangle, remove the pins.

Take a length of black floss and thread your wide eyed needle. If you struggle to get the thick thread through the eye, you can use this technique.

Cut a length of regular sewing thread (any colour).

Fold it in half and thread the folded loop through the eye of the needle.

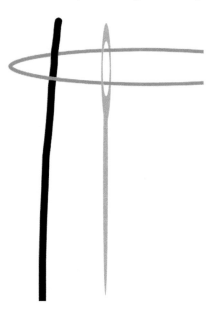

Put the end of the black cross stitch floss through the loop and pull your regular thread back through the needle. The loop of thread will pull the thicker thread back with it and thread your needle.

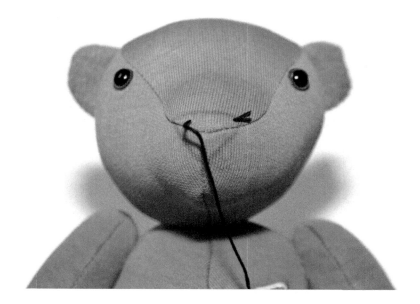

Keep the length of thread as it is and do not fold it in half and knot it to start. Simply go in and out of the space between the pencil marks, as shown. Gently and slowly pull the thread until the end of the black thread disappears inside.

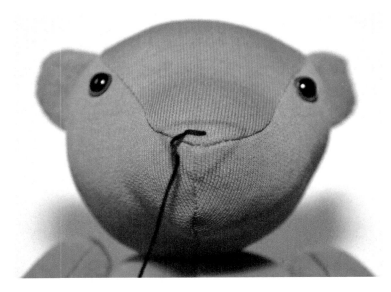

Create one stitch inside the pencil marked nose and this will anchor the thread. It will be hidden underneath the finished stitched nose.

Make one more stitch but, this time, come out with the needle at the left hand point of your pencil triangle. Make sure you are just outside the pencil mark, so it will be hidden under the stitches.

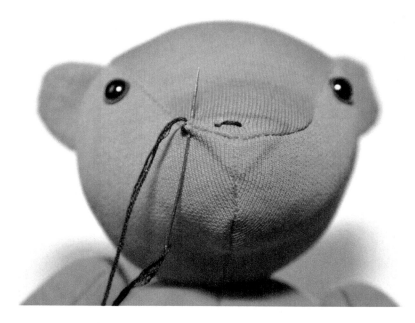

Minding your fingers, sew the bear's nose. Enter the needle at the bottom, below the pencil line and come out in a straight line above it.

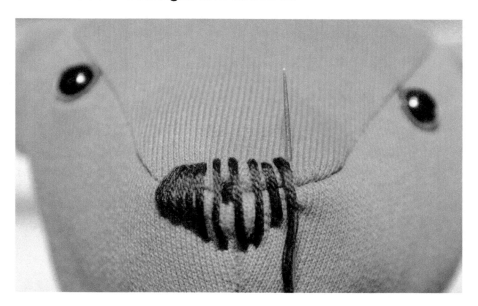

This picture shows how you will work your way along, in at the bottom and out at the top, but you will not leave any gaps between the stitches. Do not worry if you do, you can just do more stitches to cover them. If you run out of thread just start the new thread in the same way. Make sure not to pull each stitch tight, or bear will have a small lumpy nose, and that you have plenty of thread for the mouth.

To create bear's mouth, using the same black thread, you are going to sew 4 stitches in a row with no gaps between them. When you are on your last nose stitch, come out with the needle at the bottom of the bear's nose.

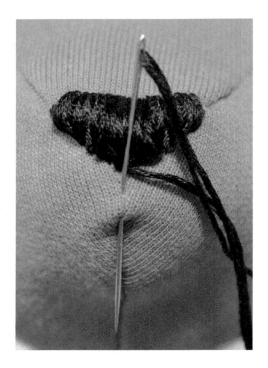

Create the next stitch as shown.

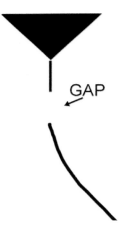

When you have pulled the thread through, you will see you have a gap.

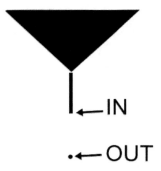

IN

OUT

You will now make your first Back Stitch. Go in and out with the needle as shown.

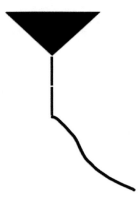

It should now look like this. Sew another normal stitch and then another back stitch.

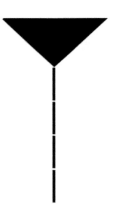

You will have 4 straight stitches with no gaps.

Now, nobody wants a grumpy bear, so it needs a happy smile.

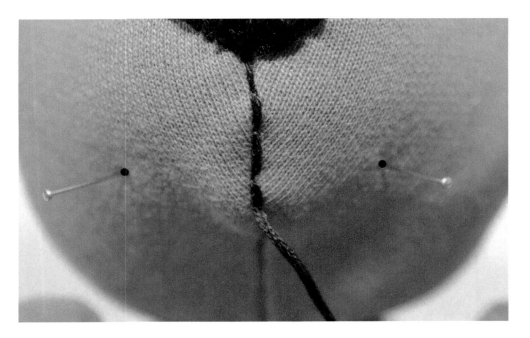

Take two pins and place them level with each other, above the line of your last stitch. Make them wider than your bear's nose.

This is what you are creating. We will start with the left side and then match the other to it. Whatever you do on one side, do the same on the other. It is just 4 stitches on each side. The thread is already in the start position.

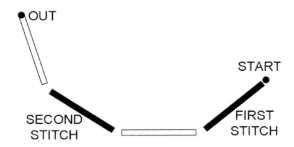

OUT

START

SECOND
STITCH

FIRST
STITCH

You are just sewing 2 stitches and leaving gaps for the other two. You can probably guess how to do the other 2 stitches, to fill in the gaps, and get back to the start point.

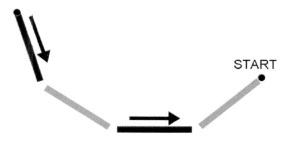

Sew the third and fourth stitches, to fill in the gaps, and come out at the start point.

Check you are happy with the way the smile looks. If not, it is easy to unpick it.

Continue to stitch the other side to match this side but stop before your last stitch.

You may prefer an older style mouth, which is a simple upside down V shape.

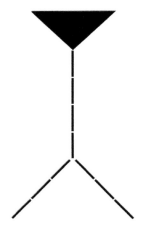

The last thing to do, with stitching the face, is to hide the end of the thread. Go down in the position to create your last stitch, but this time, go through the bear's head and out somewhere else, like a cheek. This will seem like an odd thing to do and make sure you do not lose the needle in the bear. Pick an out that is easy for you but some way from where the needle went in. Unthread the needle. Pull the thread tighter and carefully snip the thread close to the bear, so when you let go of the thread, it will disappear inside the bear. Be very careful not to cut your bear's fabric at all.

Adding the ribbon.

Choosing the colour of the ribbon can be tricky. You may want to take your new handmade bear to the shop and hold the different colours of ribbon up to it. If it has a pattern or a logo, you could choose a colour from that.

Another way is to choose the Complementary Contrast colour, which sounds complicated but it is not. It is simply the opposite colour on the colour wheel. The Primary colours are: Red, Yellow and Blue. These make up the Secondary colours: Orange, Green and Purple.

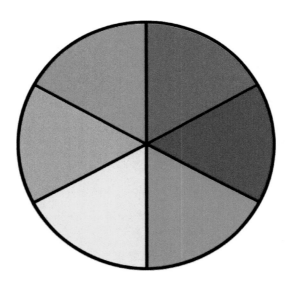

If your bear is blue then an orange would really complement it. A yellow bear would look great in purple. A red bear would suit a green ribbon.

Take your chosen length of ribbon and tie a bow around its neck. Not too tight.

When you are happy with your bow you can stitch it, behind the knot, to the bear so it does not keep coming undone.

Cut the ends of the ribbon in a V shape, as it will stop the ribbon from fraying.

Congratulations! You have completed your bear!

I hope you have enjoyed this project and that you continue to create more bears to give to others.

Wishing you many years of peaceful crafting.

Deborah Rawles

Extra pattern shapes

HEART PATTERN
PIECE

CUT 2

Extra pattern shapes

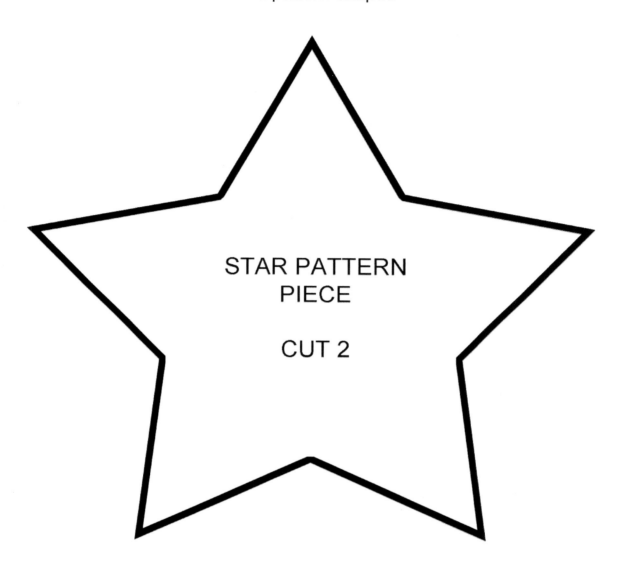

STAR PATTERN
PIECE

CUT 2

Rugby or American Football pattern.

Cut 4 of these.

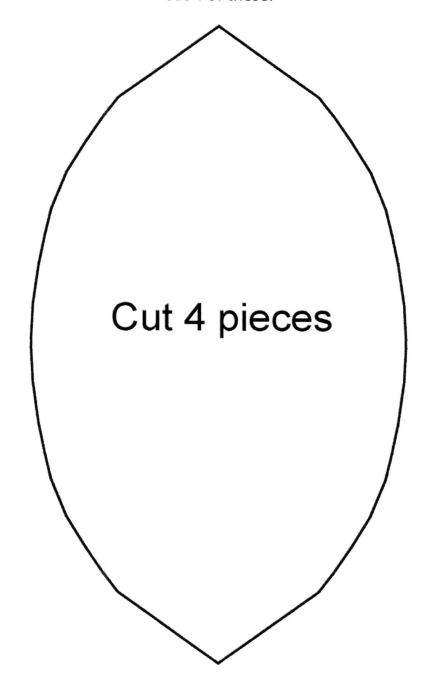

Cut 4 pieces

Other books by Deborah Rawles

1 How to make Ye Olde Toy Corner
and Card Designs

2 How to make Ye Olde
Art Studio

3 How to make Ye Olde
Antiques Corner

4 How to make Ye Olde Sweet Corner
and Jewellery Designs

5 How to make Ye Olde
Bakery Corner

6 How to make Ye Olde
Christmas Pub Corner

7 How to make Ye Olde
Chocolate Corner

How to make Ye Olde
Complete Collection

Printed in Great Britain
by Amazon

19199561R00059